Great Journeys Across Earth

CAPTAIN COOK'S PACIFIC EXPLORATIONS

Jane Bingham

Heinemann
LIBRARY

H www.heinemann.co.uk/library

Visit our website to find out more information about Heinemann Library books.

To order:

☎ Phone 44 (0) 1865 888066

🖹 Send a fax to 44 (0) 1865 314091

💻 Visit the Heinemann Bookshop at www.heinemann.co.uk/library to browse our catalogue and order online.

Produced for Heinemann Library by Monkey Puzzle Media Ltd
Gissing's Farm, Fressingfield,
Suffolk IP21 5SH, UK

First published in Great Britain by Heinemann Library, Halley Court, Jordan Hill, Oxford, OX2 8EJ, part of Harcourt Education. Heinemann is a registered trademark of Harcourt Education Ltd.

Editorial: Steve Parker and Louise Galpine
Design: Jane Hawkins and Victoria Bevan
Picture Research: Lynda Lines
Production: Severine Ribierre
Originated by Modern Age
Printed and bound in China

13 digit ISBN 978 0 431 19126 3
12 11 10 09 08
10 9 8 7 6 5 4 3 2 1

British Library Cataloguing in Publication Data
Bingham, Jane
Captain Cook's Pacific explorations. - (Great journeys across Earth)
1. Cook, James, 1728-1779 - Travel - Oceania - Juvenile literature 2. Discoveries in geography - British - History - 18th century - Juvenile literature 3. Oceania - Discovery and exploration - Juvenile literature
  I. Title
  910.9'2

Acknowledgements

akg-images pp. **14, 17** (British Library); Art Archive pp. **24, 33** (Castle Howard/Eileen Tweedy), **39**; Corbis pp. **7** (Historical Picture Archive), **19** (Robert Harding World Imagery), **23** (Stapleton Collection); FLPA p. **20** (Mitsuaki Iwago/Minden Pictures); Getty Images pp. **11** (Hulton Archive), **16** (Robert Harding World Imagery), **30** (Bill Curtsinger), **34** (Jerry Alexander), **41**; Mary Evans Picture Library pp. **9, 26**; MPM Images p. **15**; National Maritime Museum pp. **6, 27**; Nature Picture Library p. **5** (Doug Perrine); Peabody Museum of Archaeology and Ethnology pp. **36–37** (©2006 Harvard University, Peabody Museum Photo 41-72-10/499 T2360); Popperfoto.com p. **8**; Still Pictures pp. **12** (Mark Shenley), **22** (Kelvin Aitken); Topfoto pp. **1, 4, 10, 21, 28–29, 32, 40**. Maps by Martin Darlison at Encompass Graphics.

Cover photograph of Tavarua Island, Fiji, reproduced with permission of Getty Images (Ron Dahlquist).

Title page picture: Captain Cook and his party landed at Botany Bay, Australia, in April 1770.

Expert Reader: Dr Paulette Posen, environmental research scientist at the University of East Anglia

Contents

Some words are shown in bold, **like this**. You can find out what they mean by looking in the glossary.

Disaster at Sea

It was a warm, moonlit night, and the sturdy wooden ship sailed steadily north. Most of the men were asleep below deck. Even the captain was sleeping, after a busy day drawing maps of the Australian coast. Waves washed gently against the *Endeavour*'s sides and a light wind blew.

Suddenly, the peace was shattered. With a deafening crack, the *Endeavour* shuddered to a halt, and there was a terrible sound of splintering wood. The sailors rushed to the side of the ship and peered down into the water. In the pale moonlight, they saw broken planks of wood floating on the waves.

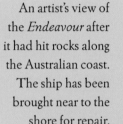

An artist's view of the *Endeavour* after it had hit rocks along the Australian coast. The ship has been brought near to the shore for repair.

Captain Cook takes charge

In minutes, Captain Cook was up on deck, still dressed in his nightshirt. He told the crew to keep very calm. Then he gave orders to start pumping water out of the ship's hold (the lower part where the main cargo is stored). He also sent an officer in a small rowing boat to inspect the damage.

The Great Barrier Reef

The Endeavour's accident happened when it hit the Great Barrier Reef. This massive shelf of hardened coral stretches along the northeast coast of Australia for over 1,500 km (1,000 miles). Coral reefs are formed from the skeletons of millions of tiny sea creatures, which all stick together to form a rocky mass.

The Great Barrier Reef is made from many types of coral rocks. It teems with thousands of fish and other wildlife.

The officer returned with dreadful news. The ship's **hull** had been pierced by a sharp spear of **coral**. Even more worrying, the *Endeavour* was stuck fast on a coral **reef**. Unless the ship could be floated off very soon, it might be smashed to pieces by the waves.

What had brought a British ship to the other side of the world? And why were all the men on board risking their lives?

Hole in the hull

Joseph Banks, a scientist on board the *Endeavour*, wrote about the shipwreck in his diary:

"Our situation now became greatly alarming ... we were upon sunken coral rocks, the most dreadful of all others on account of their sharp points and grinding quality, which cut through the ship's bottom almost immediately..."

Getting Ready

Captain Cook's voyage had begun two years earlier, in 1768, when his ship set sail from England. At this time, most of his crew believed that their journey would end at Tahiti, a small island in the South Pacific Ocean. In fact, this was just the starting point for their adventures.

Observing Venus

When Cook left England, people thought he was going to study the night sky. The planet Venus was due to pass in front of the Sun and Cook's job was to record the planet's movements. His look-out point was the island of Tahiti. However, this was not his final destination.

A secret plan

Unknown to the crew, Cook had secret orders from the British Royal Navy. After he had observed the planet Venus, he was to keep sailing south. In the second part of his voyage, he was to search for the mysterious Great Southern Land.

Eighteenth-century **navigators** relied on detailed knowledge of the Sun, Moon, and stars. They used simple navigation instruments to plot their ship's course.

Studying the stars

Cook's expedition to observe the planet Venus was paid for by the **Royal Society**. This was a group of scientists who were fascinated by **astronomy**. The science of astronomy was also very useful to ships' captains. By studying the sky at night, they could use the stars to help them steer their course.

In the 1770s, many people believed that there was a vast land mass or **continent** in the South Pacific Ocean. This was often known as the Great Southern Land. Britain, France, and Holland all wanted to claim it as their own, so they could explore it for gold, spices, and other riches. But the British were determined to be first, so they kept their plans quiet.

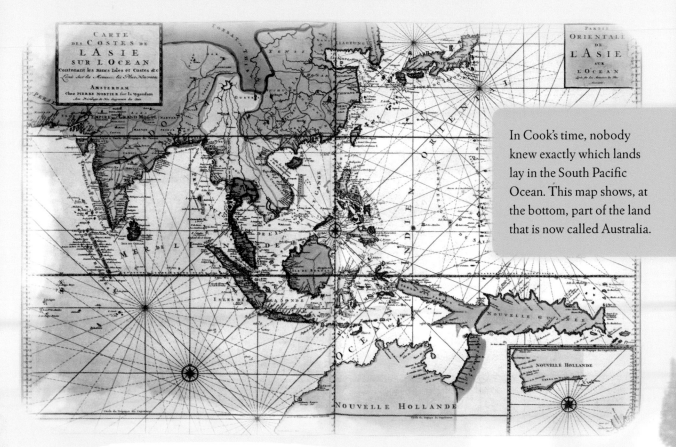

In Cook's time, nobody knew exactly which lands lay in the South Pacific Ocean. This map shows, at the bottom, part of the land that is now called Australia.

The search for the Great Southern Land

For over a century before Cook's voyage, people had tried to find the Great Southern Land. In 1642 Dutch explorer Abel Tasman reached the west coast of New Zealand and was sure that he had found its edge. Later, several sailors in the South Pacific reported seeing large masses of land. These possible glimpses were exciting, but not solid proof. Cook's task was to find and map the mysterious continent.

Finding a captain

The expedition to the Pacific needed a very special leader, and there was one obvious choice. James Cook was 39 years old and an experienced captain in the Royal Navy. He had fought in sea battles and produced a detailed map of the coast of Newfoundland, in northeast Canada. He was also eager for adventure. Captain Cook was the perfect man to lead the search for the Great Southern Land.

Cook's early life

James Cook was the son of a farm worker from the north of England. After he left school, he worked in a grocer's shop, then he went to sea at the age of 18. For the next eight years, he worked on a coal-carrying ship, and learned the skills of sailing the hard way. This was great preparation for his later adventures.

A second-hand ship

Cook chose his ship very carefully. It had to be very strong to cope with storms, and large enough to hold plenty of supplies. It also needed a wide, flat **hull** so it could sail in shallow waters. Cook decided on a sturdy "cat" – a coal-carrying ship like the ones he had worked on when he first went to sea. The navy soon found a second-hand cat and prepared it specially for the voyage.

By the 1770s, James Cook had 20 years' experience at sea. He was also a skilled astronomer and map-maker.

Finding a crew

After he had chosen his ship, Cook's next task was to gather his crew. This was made up mainly of sailors, but there were also carpenters, a surgeon, and a cook. Altogether, there were more than 80 men on board. Some of them had sailed with Cook before, and some had already been on voyages around the world.

The *Endeavour*
Cook's ship was named the Endeavour. To "endeavour" means to try as hard as you can, even when things get difficult. It turned out to be the perfect name for his ship.

As the *Endeavour* set sail from Britain, it flew the Red Ensign, the flag of the Royal Navy.

Ship's supplies

Cook decided that the *Endeavour* should set sail from Plymouth, a busy port on Britain's southwest coast. Here, the ship was loaded with fresh water, food, tools, wood, and other supplies. Stacked inside the *Endeavour*'s hold were large quantities of dry biscuits and salted meat. Cook also ordered dozens of jars of pickled cabbage. He believed that it could help prevent a terrible disease called **scurvy**.

Scurvy sailors

In the 18th century, sailors on long voyages suffered from a horrible disease called scurvy. This was caused by a lack of vitamin C, found in fresh fruit and vegetables. Sailors with scurvy developed spots on their legs and their teeth fell out.

Cook was one of the few captains who worked out how to cure scurvy. In this picture, a sick sailor is fed fresh fruit.

Joseph Banks, naturalist

When Cook reached Plymouth, a message was waiting from the scientists of the Royal Society. It told him to expect an important passenger. This was Joseph Banks, a wealthy young man who was very interested in animals, plants, rocks, and the study of **natural history**.

Banks' aim was to record all the animals and plants found on the voyage. He brought along his secretary, four servants, and the Swedish **naturalist** Doctor Daniel Solander. Banks also invited two artists to join him on their great expedition. These were Alexander Buchan, who painted views and landscapes, and Sydney Parkinson, who was skilled at drawing animals and plants.

Ship's goat

Apart from captain and crew, scientists and artists, the *Endeavour* had a ship's goat. It provided fresh milk for the sailors. The goat was a very experienced sailor. It had already made one voyage around the world!

Banks' baggage

Joseph Banks had dozens of books, fishing nets, and jars, and an underwater telescope. He also had a strange machine for catching small animals by stunning them with a small electric shock. He also tried the shocks on people!

Joseph Banks was only 25 when he joined the *Endeavour*, but he was determined to be a famous naturalist.

The Voyage Begins

On 25 August 1768, the *Endeavour* left Plymouth and headed south. At first, the weather was stormy. Then the seas became calmer as the ship approached Madeira, an island off the northwest coast of Africa. There the crew spent a happy week, while Joseph Banks recorded the island's wildlife.

Crossing the Atlantic

After leaving Madeira, the *Endeavour* crossed the Atlantic Ocean, heading for South America. This voyage lasted for eight weeks, and the weather was mostly good. On this part of the trip, Cook ordered a sailor to be whipped, as punishment for refusing to eat fresh food. Many men on board were shocked by his strictness. But Cook wanted his crew to stay as fit and healthy as possible.

Crossing the Equator

*Before the Endeavour reached South America, it crossed the **Equator**, an imaginary line running around the centre of Earth. The sailors held a **ceremony** to mark this event. Anyone who had not crossed the Equator before had to be dunked in the ocean three times, or pay a fine to avoid a soaking.*

Land of Fire

The first stop in South America was Rio de Janeiro, Brazil. Cook stocked up on supplies and continued south to the island of Tierra del Fuego ("Land of Fire"), at the tip of South America. The crew rested for six days, gathering fresh food. They noted that the local people lived in huts made from branches covered with sealskins. They lit large fires to keep themselves warm, giving the name "Land of Fire".

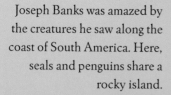

Joseph Banks was amazed by the creatures he saw along the coast of South America. Here, seals and penguins share a rocky island.

Rounding the Cape

Cook then faced the challenge of sailing round the tip of South America, which is called Cape Horn. This was a terrifying experience, as the little ship battled against violent winds and huge waves. But finally the *Endeavour* reached the Pacific Ocean.

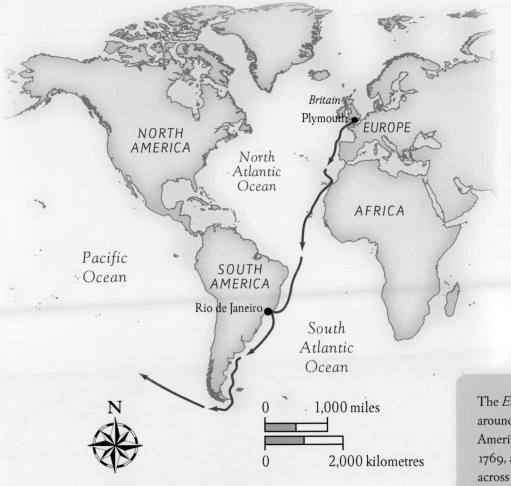

The *Endeavour* sailed around the tip of South America at the start of 1769, and headed out across the Pacific Ocean.

Magellan's voyage

The first European to travel around the tip of South America was Portuguese explorer Ferdinand Magellan. In 1520, he sailed through a channel of water that was later named the Strait of Magellan.

Reaching Tahiti

Once the *Endeavour* had left Cape Horn, it sailed through empty seas for three months. At last, it reached Tahiti. All the crew were delighted by this tropical paradise, with long, sandy beaches fringed by palm trees. As their ship approached the shore, they were welcomed by friendly islanders in wooden canoes, loaded with fruit, coconuts, and fish.

Tahitian tattoos

The explorers were fascinated by tattoo-like patterns on the Tahitians' bodies. These were made by piercing the skin using a bone instrument with many sharp teeth, and rubbing in a bluish-black dye, made by burning oily nuts.

Staying on the island

The *Endeavour* stayed at Tahiti for about three months. Captain Cook and the ship's astronomer, Charles Green, made their observations of the planet Venus. Banks and Cook described how they joined in feasts, listened to Tahitian drums and pipes, and watched religious ceremonies performed on *morai*. The *morai* were sacred platforms carved from **coral** and stone.

The islanders of Tahiti called the patterns on their skin *tatau*.

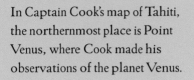

In Captain Cook's map of Tahiti, the northernmost place is Point Venus, where Cook made his observations of the planet Venus.

Tupia and Tayeto

When the *Endeavour* left Tahiti, it carried two new passengers. They were Tupia, a Tahitian priest, and his young assistant Tayeto. Tupia was welcomed on board as an expert **navigator**. Later, he made friends with many of the people they met on the voyage.

South Sea sailors

Like many South Pacific islanders, Tupia could navigate without scientific instruments. The Pacific islanders steered their canoes using their knowledge of their environment. They navigated by studying the position of the stars, the flight patterns of birds, and the direction of ocean currents and winds.

The Society Islands

*Cook gave the name Society Islands to the group of islands that contain Tahiti. Some people say this was in honour of the **Royal Society**. Other people say that Cook chose the name because the islands were very close together, and so very "social".*

Meeting the Maoris

Once the *Endeavour* left the Society Islands, Cook prepared to search for the Great Southern Land. Everyone on board began to realize they were not going home just yet, and several sailors became very angry. Cook's orders were to head directly south from Tahiti, in search of the new land. However, after a month of sailing south, no land was sighted. So Cook decided it was time to change direction.

Heading west

Cook's new plan was to explore the eastern side of New Zealand. When the Dutch explorer Abel Tasman had visited New Zealand in the 1640s he had only seen its western coast. No one had any idea how large New Zealand was, and if it could be the mysterious Great Southern Land.

The *Endeavour* sailed west for a month, until a young sailor lookout yelled out "Land ahoy!". Cook's charts told him that he had reached the east coast of New Zealand.

A bad beginning

The ship anchored in a large bay, and Cook and some sailors went ashore in two small boats. Cook had already spotted some Maoris, the local people of New Zealand, and was keen to make friends. Some sailors were left to guard the boats, while Cook led another group farther inland. But before he got very far, he heard a gunshot. One of the boat guards had killed a Maori man. This was a bad start.

The Maori people are famous for their dramatic woodcarvings, like this painted figure from a Maori graveyard.

Young Nick's Head
Cook named the place where the Endeavour landed "Young Nick's Head". Nick was the name of the sailor who had first spotted land. He was only 12 or 13 years old.

A terrible day

The following morning, around a hundred Maoris gathered at the place where their companion died. They performed a terrifying war dance as the British approached. Cook tried to show that he wanted peace, but another Maori was killed by the explorers. Later that day, a war canoe approached the *Endeavour* with Maoris throwing stones, and four of them were shot.

Disagreeable deeds
Joseph Banks was horrified by the Maoris' deaths. He described his second day on New Zealand as "the most disagreeable day my life has yet seen".

Before going into battle, Maori warriors perform *haka*, jumping into the air and pulling angry faces. Cook's crew were terrified by this ferocious war dance.

Talking to the Maoris

The Maoris never really welcomed the explorers. But later, a few of them made friends with Cook's crew. This was mainly thanks to Tupia, the priest from Tahiti. To everyone's amazement, Tupia could talk easily with the Maoris in their language.

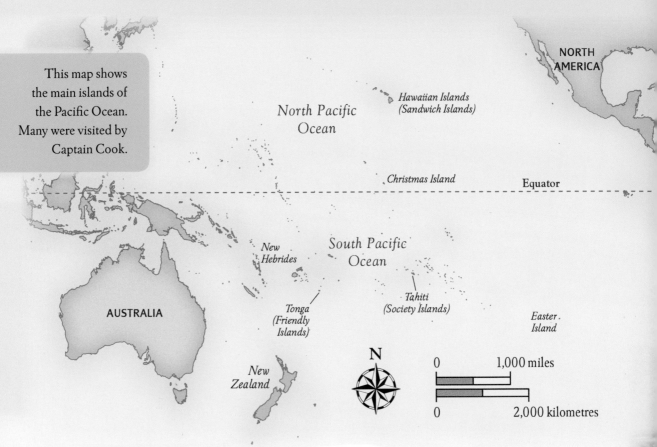

This map shows the main islands of the Pacific Ocean. Many were visited by Captain Cook.

NORTH AMERICA

North Pacific Ocean

Hawaiian Islands (Sandwich Islands)

Christmas Island

Equator

New Hebrides

South Pacific Ocean

AUSTRALIA

Tonga (Friendly Islands)

Tahiti (Society Islands)

Easter Island

New Zealand

N

0   1,000 miles

0   2,000 kilometres

Pacific peoples

Even though Tupia came from the faraway island of Tahiti, he was able to talk to the Maoris. Their languages had words and phrases in common. Around 6,000 years ago, some people in Southeast Asia sailed in search of new land. Gradually, they spread to islands across the Pacific. Their languages changed in some details over the years. But certain words, sayings, and phrases stayed much the same.

Several members of the crew described the Maoris in their diaries. They were very impressed by the warriors' swirling tattoos, which looked very different from the simple patterns of the Tahitian tattoos. The explorers also described the Maoris' fine carvings and their ornaments made from **jade**. Joseph Banks noted that the usual Maori greeting was to rub noses with each other.

Charting the coast

Once Cook had stocked up with fresh food and water, he was keen to start charting the coast of New Zealand. He made his way slowly round North Island, drawing maps as he went.

At the southern tip of North Island, Cook saw land to the south. For a while, he thought this was part of a vast country. However, as he continued, he realized it was another island. By March 1770, Cook had charted the North and South islands of New Zealand. He had also shown that this was not the Great Southern Land.

Men or monsters?
The visit of Captain Cook and his crew later became a legend among the Maori people. In their stories, the Maoris described some monsters who arrived on their shore. The monsters rowed their boats backwards, as if they had eyes in the backs of their heads.

Separation Point lies between Golden Bay and Tasman Bay on the north coast of New Zealand's South Island.

Australian Adventures

Before Captain Cook left the South Pacific, there was one more country he wanted to explore. This was the land known as New Holland, which would later be called Australia.

Tasmania or Van Diemen's Land?

The island of Tasmania was given two names by Europeans. In 1642 Abel Tasman named it Van Diemen's Land after the powerful man who paid for his voyage. In 1856, the island was renamed Tasmania in honour of Tasman.

New Holland and Van Diemen's Land

European sailors had known about New Holland since the 1640s, but their ideas about it were very vague. In 1644, Abel Tasman (the Dutch explorer who reached New Zealand) had caught sight of the northwest coast of Australia. Tasman called this land New Holland, but he did not explore it. Over the next hundred years, other explorers charted parts of New Holland's western coast. But nobody had any idea how large this place was.

In Australia, Banks recorded dozens of wildlife species previously unknown to Europeans. One of these species was the grey kangaroo, shown here.

Reaching New Holland

Cook was determined to clear up the mystery of New Holland, so he set sail for Tasmania. However, strong winds carried him farther north, to a different shore. Cook soon realized that he had found a coast no European had ever seen before. He suspected that this must be the eastern side of the vast country of New Holland.

Cook gave orders to sail north and look for somewhere to land. Eventually, he found a large bay and the crew went ashore. They were the first Europeans to set foot in eastern Australia.

Botany Bay

*Cook gave the name **Botany** Bay to the place where the explorers went ashore. Botany is the study of plants, and the bay was a wonderful place to find new plants and flowers. It was home to an astonishing range of **species** that had never been seen in Europe.*

This artist's impression shows Cook landing in Botany Bay, Australia, with **Aboriginal** hunters in the distance.

Exploring Australia

The *Endeavour* stayed for a week in Botany Bay. Then it continued northwards, as Cook mapped the coast. The ship made many stops and the crew had plenty of chances to explore. They were all delighted by the Australian wildlife – especially the kangaroos, turtles, and parrots.

Cook's crew often spotted turtles on the Australian shore. Sometimes they captured them for meat. Today all sea turtles are protected by law, in all parts of the world.

Skipping Sydney

*Soon after leaving Botany Bay, Cook passed an **inlet** in the coast. He named it Port Jackson but did not explore it. In fact, the inlet led to one of the world's best natural ports, which later became Sydney Harbour.*

Aboriginal people

Most of the time, the Aboriginal Australians kept away from the strangers on their shores. But the explorers noted that the Aboriginals were tall and strong, and had white patterns painted on their bodies. The explorers also described how the Aboriginal hunters used spears and **boomerangs** to catch their prey.

This painting shows Aboriginal people in bark canoes. It was made by Sydney Parkinson, one of the artists on board the *Endeavour*.

A narrow escape

The voyage up the coast went very smoothly until the terrible night when the *Endeavour* struck the Great Barrier **Reef**. For 24 hours, the crew faced death, as they waited helplessly for the tide to lift their ship off the rocks.

At last, the following night, the *Endeavour* floated free. However, the trouble was still far from over. The hole in the **hull** was letting in water fast. Fortunately one of the crew, Jonathan Monkhouse, had faced this situation before. He quickly explained how to patch up the ship using cloth from the sails.

The Aboriginals

People who have lived in the same place for a very long time are known as the aboriginals or "original people" in that region. In Australia, this term has been used for the name of the original Australian people themselves. But it is usually written with a capital A, as Aboriginals (or Aborigines).

Leaving Australia

Once the sailors had patched up the hole, Cook steered his ship towards a sandy beach. Then the *Endeavour* was checked for damage. It was much worse than Cook had feared. Apart from the massive hole in the hull, worms had attacked most of its timbers.

Cook decided it was time to head for home. As soon as the ship was safe to sail, he continued up the Australian coast to its northernmost point. Then he sailed west towards the Dutch East Indies.

Stopping in Java

In October 1770 the *Endeavour* arrived in the port of Batavia on the island of Java. A crowd of Dutch settlers had gathered to greet the ship. They were the first Europeans the crew had seen for over two years.

This view of Batavia, in the East Indies, shows how it looked in Cook's time. It is now Jakarta, the capital of Indonesia.

The East indies

The East Indies were a group of islands in present-day Indonesia. Many were claimed by Dutch or Portuguese settlers in the 17th century, and became valuable trading bases. The islands were rich in spices such as cinnamon and nutmeg, and they were often known as the Spice Islands.

It took two months to prepare the *Endeavour* for the voyage home. Sadly, Batavia was a very unhealthy place. Many of the crew caught **malaria**, while others suffered from **dysentery**. More than 40 died from these diseases, including Tupia and Tayeto.

Cook's first voyage took more than three years, from 1768 to 1771.

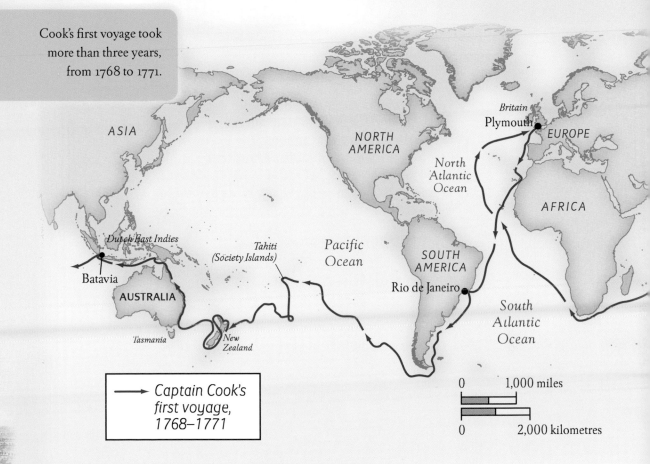

ASIA

NORTH AMERICA

Britain
Plymouth
EUROPE

North Atlantic Ocean

AFRICA

Dutch East Indies

Batavia

Tahiti (Society Islands)

Pacific Ocean

SOUTH AMERICA

Rio de Janeiro

South Atlantic Ocean

AUSTRALIA

Tasmania

New Zealand

⟶ Captain Cook's first voyage, 1768–1771

0   1,000 miles

0   2,000 kilometres

Returning home

After leaving Batavia, the crew still had to face another six months at sea. Finally on 13 July 1771, they arrived back in Britain. Large crowds gathered to welcome the *Endeavour*. Captain Cook was a national hero, but Joseph Banks claimed most of the glory. He became a **celebrity**, and toured the country showing off his collections of animals and plants.

Expedition to Antarctica

After just a few months at home, Captain Cook began to prepare for his next voyage. He wanted to have one more try at finding the Great Southern Land. This time he planned to sail much farther south and explore the icy frozen seas around **Antarctica**.

Antarctica

*The **continent** of Antarctica is a vast area of frozen land around the South Pole. It makes up one-tenth of Earth's land surface, and has several mountain ranges. The average temperature in the middle of Antarctica is well below freezing, at -50°C (-58°F). Whales, seals, penguins, and other sea birds live there.*

Resolution and Adventure

For his second voyage, Cook decided to take two ships. Just like the *Endeavour*, these were second-hand, and had originally carried coal. They were renamed the *Resolution* and the *Adventure*.

The *Resolution* and the *Adventure* began their voyage together, but later they were often separated.

Cook was captain of the *Resolution*. The second captain was Tobias Furneaux, an experienced officer who had already sailed to Tahiti. As well as the usual crew, both ships carried **naturalists**, astronomers, and artists.

On 13 July 1772, the *Resolution* and *Adventure* set off from Plymouth. They stopped in Madeira and South Africa, before heading south to the Antarctic.

Trouble with Banks

The naturalist Joseph Banks had planned to join the second expedition. But he was now famous and expected to travel in style. He ordered extra cabins to be built on the *Resolution*. However the cabins made the ship unsafe and were torn down. When Banks saw the cabins he would have to use, he refused to join the expedition.

A copy of the chronometer (or "sea clock") used by Cook on his second and third voyages.

A sea clock

*When Cook set off for Antarctica, he had a brand new navigation instrument on board. This was the **chronometer**, a very precise clock, which could keep time even on a swaying, storm-lashed ship. Using a chronometer, **navigators** could keep exact records of their positions and plan a more accurate course.*

Heading south

Within a few days of leaving South Africa, the ships were battling against icy winds. All the men were given heavy canvas suits and woolly hats, but they were soon covered with ice. Icicles hung from the sailors' noses and their hands often froze to the ship's ropes.

By December, the two captains were steering a dangerous course between tall icebergs. To make things even harder, the weather was often foggy. One very foggy day, the ships lost sight of each other. The *Resolution* had to sail on alone.

Iced water

In Antarctica, Cook made an interesting discovery. He found that water from melted icebergs was not salty, as most of his crew expected. Instead, it was fresh and good for drinking. This is because icebergs are made from snow, and not from frozen sea water.
The discovery meant that the sailors were never short of fresh water while they were among icebergs.

Wonderful waterspouts
*In New Zealand, the explorers were amazed to see tall columns of water spurting out of the sea. These waterspouts are similar to **tornadoes** or "twisters" on land. They are caused by powerful spinning winds that whip up the surface of the ocean.*

Turning north

Cook continued sailing south until February. By this time his crew was exhausted and he decided to turn north. The *Resolution* reached New Zealand's South Island in late March 1773. After resting there, Cook sailed up the coast to the North Island, where he met up again with the *Adventure*.

Tahiti and Tonga

When both ships were loaded with fresh supplies, Cook set out eastwards into the South Pacific. He was heading for Tahiti again, but also searching for more islands on the way. The explorers spent a happy month on Tahiti before sailing west to the islands of Tonga. Cook had such a warm welcome from the Tongan people that he named their lands the Friendly Islands.

This painting shows *Resolution* and *Adventure* at anchor in Matavai Bay, Tahiti.

Return to Antarctica

After his stay on Tonga, Captain Cook decided it was time to head south again. The two ships set off for New Zealand, but they were separated on the way. Cook waited a month at their meeting place. Then he decided to continue alone.

As the *Resolution* sailed south, the weather rapidly grew colder. Soon the ship was surrounded by mountainous icebergs, but Cook kept sailing. At the end of January 1774, the *Resolution* finally met a sheet of solid ice. Cook had voyaged further south than anyone before, but now he had to turn back.

In Antarctica, the sailors were amazed by the sight of hundreds of penguins standing on icebergs.

Antarctica

Captain Cook wrote in his diary about Antarctica:

"I ... had ambitions not only to go further than anyone had done before, but as far as it was possible for man to go."

Easter Island

Six weeks later, Cook arrived at Easter Island. As their ship approached the shore, the crew were frightened by huge stone figures staring out to sea. However, they soon discovered that the Easter Islanders were gentle and friendly.

The voyage home

After Easter Island, Cook stopped at several other islands before returning to New Zealand. There he prepared to return home. For the first part of this voyage, he stayed quite far south. He sailed through almost empty seas, although he did reach the small island of South Georgia.

Finally, Cook reached a point in the ocean directly south of Africa. Then he turned north and headed for home. He had explored all the southern parts of the Pacific Ocean, and showed that the Great Southern Land did not exist.

News from New Zealand

The Adventure *returned to Britain a year before the* Resolution, *with a frightening tale. The ship had finally reached New Zealand, but soon after that, 11 men were lost. A search party was sent to look for the missing men. It discovered that they had been eaten by cannibals.*

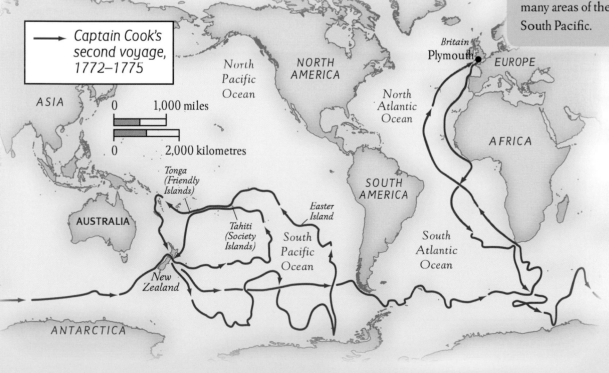

Cook's second voyage included many areas of the South Pacific.

Cook's Last Voyage

After his second voyage, James Cook settled down at home. For a while he was quite content. But then he heard of plans for a new voyage of exploration.

Looking north

Following Cook's travels in the South Pacific, the British were keen to find new lands in the North Pacific. They also hoped to claim some land on the western coast of North America. Most of all, the British wanted to explore the northwest coast of Canada. They longed to find a much easier sailing route to Eastern lands, which they called the Northwest Passage.

At the time, the sailing route from Europe to the East was long and dangerous. Ships had to sail around South America or South Africa. Explorers before Cook had tried to find the Northwest Passage across the top of North America, but failed. If this link between the North Pacific and North Atlantic Oceans was proved to exist, it would become a very important shipping route.

Setting off

Cook volunteered to be the leader of the new expedition. On 12 July 1776, he set sail once again in the *Resolution*, and he was soon joined by the *Discovery*. The captain of the *Discovery* was Charles Clerke, an officer on Cook's two earlier voyages.

An officer on the *Resolution* was William Bligh. Later, as captain of the *Bounty*, he faced a famous uprising. His crew took over and cast Bligh and a few followers adrift in a small boat. Bligh made it back to England, was cleared by a court, and rose to the rank of vice admiral.

A Noah's ark

Cook called his ship a "Noah's ark" because it was so packed with animals. King George III had instructed Cook to give these animals to the people he visited. They included sheep, rabbits, pigs, cows, horses, and a magnificent peacock and peahen.

Return to the South Pacific

The two ships headed first for the islands of the South Pacific. Here, Cook had the job of returning a Society Islander to his home. Omai had been brought to Britain on the *Resolution*. Now he was going home with many treasures, including a suit of armour!

The handsome Society Islander, Omai, became a **celebrity** in London. This portrait is by the famous English artist Sir Joshua Reynolds.

New land ahoy!

Cook's expedition sailed into the North Pacific Ocean in early December 1777. On 24 December, Christmas Eve, he reached a small island, which he named Christmas Island. Then on 18 January 1778, the shout came again: "Land ahoy!". Soon, Cook could see several high mountains. He was approaching the Hawaiian Islands.

The mountainous Hawaiian island of Kauai still looks much the same today as it did in Cook's time.

The islands of Hawaii

Hawaii is the name for a group of eight main islands and many smaller islets in the North Pacific. It is also the name of the largest of these islands. Captain Cook called the group the Sandwich Islands after the Earl of Sandwich, the commander of the British Royal Navy. But this name was only used until the 1890s. Hawaii is now a state of the United States.

An island welcome

Next morning the two ships reached the island of Kauai. A group of islanders paddled out in long canoes to greet them. The Hawaiians were happy to trade, offering pigs and sweet potatoes in exchange for iron nails.

The explorers soon discovered that the Hawaiians could understand some South Pacific words. It showed that these islanders, like the Tahitians, belonged to the same main group of people who had spread out from South Asia thousands of years before.

Exploring Kauai

Cook ordered his ships to anchor in Waimea Bay, and the crew spent the next few weeks on Kauai. They were impressed by the tall, carved wooden figures that stood guard over the island's holy places. They also admired the Hawaiian women's hip-swaying "hula" dancing. After leaving Kauai, Cook visited the island of Niihau, but he was keen to press on and soon set sail again. He wanted to reach North America and search for the legendary Northwest Passage.

Riding the waves

British sailors always kept well away from breaking waves, so they were amazed to see the Hawaiians riding the surf. The islanders used narrow wooden planks, much like surfers today.

Reaching North America

Cook sighted western North America on 6 March 1778. The weather was wild and stormy as the ships battled north along what is now the Oregon coast, looking for a place to land. Eventually they reached a sheltered bay, Nootka Sound, close to present-day Vancouver Island.

Meeting Native Americans

In Nootka Sound, Cook was met by warriors in large wooden canoes. Once they reached the British ships, the warriors all stood up, drummed their paddles against the sides of their canoe, and chanted loudly to welcome the strangers. The sailors quickly noticed that Nootka Sound was filled with birds. As well as ducks and gulls, the explorers spotted hummingbirds, albatrosses, and bald eagles.

This picture of a Nootka "longhouse" was copied from a sketch by one of Cook's crew. The ceiling racks are for drying fish.

The explorers stayed at Nootka for a month, gathering supplies and repairing their ships. They visited the long, wooden houses of the local people, and were astonished by their carved totem poles and fierce animal masks.

In Alaska, the sailors traded with Inuit people, who gave them heavy furs to keep warm. Then they sailed through the Bering Strait – the narrow area of sea that separates Asia from North America.

Now Cook had reached the frozen **Arctic** region. He still hoped to find a northern passage east, into the Atlantic Ocean. But near the end of August, his ships met a blank wall of ice. It was time to head back to the Pacific Ocean.

The Arctic
The Arctic is a vast icy region around the North Pole. It is mostly frozen ocean, but some lands, such as Canada, jut into it. The average temperature falls to around -34°C (-29°F).

Horror on Hawaii

Cook was back in the Hawaiian Islands by November. This time he sailed past Maui and headed for Hawaii, where he anchored in Kealakekua Bay.

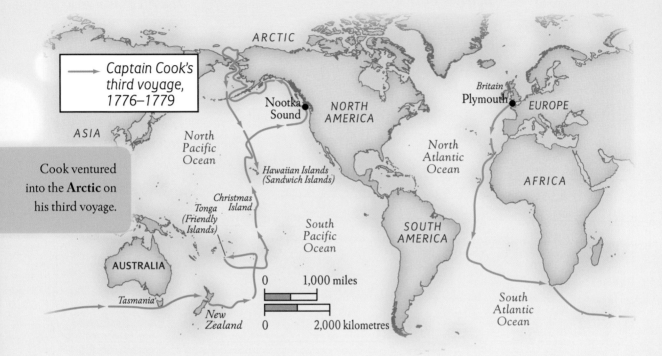

Captain Cook's third voyage, 1776–1779

Cook ventured into the **Arctic** on his third voyage.

Welcoming a god

A priest called Koa arrived by canoe at Cook's ship. He wrapped a red cloak around the captain's shoulders and took him ashore. Cook was greeted by hundreds of islanders who believed he was their great god, Lono. The islanders threw themselves to the ground and held a welcome **ceremony**.

For the next three weeks, Cook and his crew were given lavish gifts. Then the islanders made it clear that it was time for them to go. Cook left Hawaii in a solemn ceremony, but within four days he was back. His ships had been damaged in a storm and needed repairs. However, this time Cook was not welcome. Legend said that Lono was not supposed to return, and the islanders were tired of entertaining the greedy crew.

Lono the god

Lono was one of the most important Hawaiian gods. He had promised his people that one day he would return in a large canoe. So, when the islanders saw Cook's boat, they believed he was Lono.

Violent death

After a few quarrels between the islanders and the crew, Cook decided to talk to the island's chief. He took a guard of armed men. But as the meeting started, some Hawaiian warriors attacked Cook's guards. The guards ran off to their boat, leaving the captain alone.

Cook turned and walked slowly towards the shore. After only a few steps, a warrior struck him on the head with a heavy club. The captain fell to his knees, and another islander plunged a dagger into his neck. Soon Cook was surrounded by warriors, battering him to death. It was a tragic end for a great explorer.

A changed man

On his third voyage, Cook often gave strange orders. His decision to return to Hawaii was one of the many mistakes he made. Perhaps he was exhausted after all his travels.

This picture shows Cook's final moments in Kealakekua Bay. He is surrounded by angry Hawaiians, while his guards try to defend him from their boats.

Captain Cook's Legacy

Captain James Cook was one of the world's greatest **navigators**. He created accurate maps of all the lands he visited and was recognized as an outstanding explorer. The places he visited were never the same again. Some people think this was a good thing, but others disagree.

Australia and New Zealand

Cook is especially famous for reaching Australia. Within 20 years, the first settlers began to arrive from Britain, and Australia soon became a British **colony**. New Zealand was also settled by the British. Even today, Australia and New Zealand have very strong links with Britain.

Health care

Unlike most captains of his time, Cook managed to keep a very healthy crew. Apart from insisting that they eat fresh fruit and vegetables, to ward off **scurvy**, he ordered them to wash frequently and keep their ship clean. Cook's methods were copied by other captains. His ideas saved many lives.

Cook the hero: this monument to the great explorer is in Poverty Bay, North Island, the place where he first came ashore in New Zealand.

Animals and plants

During Cook's journeys, **naturalists** recorded many new **species** of animals and plants. These discoveries added greatly to people's understanding of the natural world. The naturalists' records also helped scientists to make many advances in the study of **botany** and **zoology**.

Opening up the Pacific

As well as exploring many southern Pacific islands, Cook was the first European to reach the Hawaiian Islands. When people back home heard of Cook's voyages, many ships arrived in the Pacific carrying traders, settlers, and missionaries. All these people had a dramatic impact on the islanders' way of life.

The Aboriginal view

*Cook is not a hero to everyone. Some Australian **Aboriginals** accuse Cook of stealing their country. The Maoris of New Zealand and the native Hawaiians also have mixed feelings about Cook. Many of them see him as the person who began the process of changing their culture.*

A different view: Aboriginal Australians protest about the treatment of their people, on the anniversary of the arrival of the first European settlers.

Three Pacific Adventures

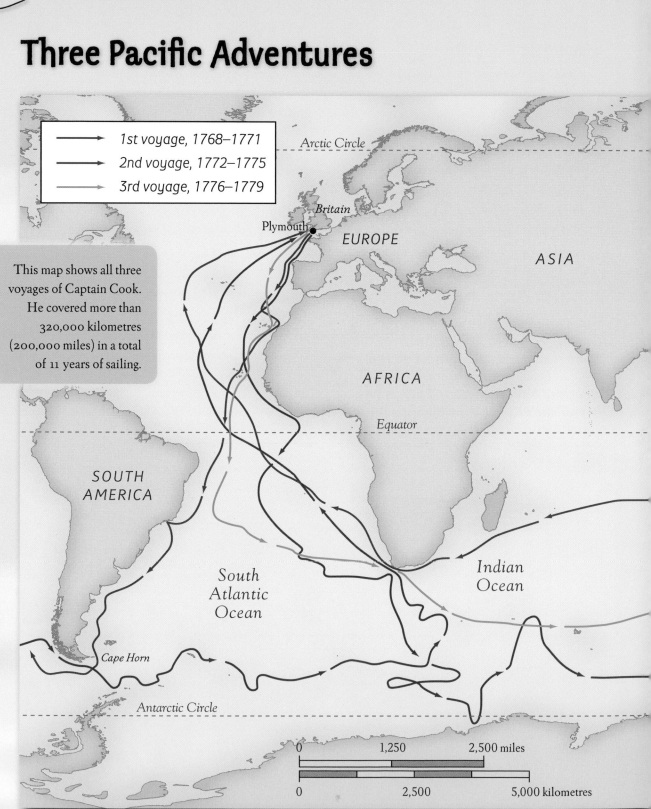

Legend:
- 1st voyage, 1768–1771
- 2nd voyage, 1772–1775
- 3rd voyage, 1776–1779

Arctic Circle

Britain

Plymouth

EUROPE

ASIA

This map shows all three voyages of Captain Cook. He covered more than 320,000 kilometres (200,000 miles) in a total of 11 years of sailing.

AFRICA

Equator

SOUTH AMERICA

South Atlantic Ocean

Indian Ocean

Cape Horn

Antarctic Circle

| 0 | 1,250 | 2,500 miles |

| 0 | 2,500 | 5,000 kilometres |

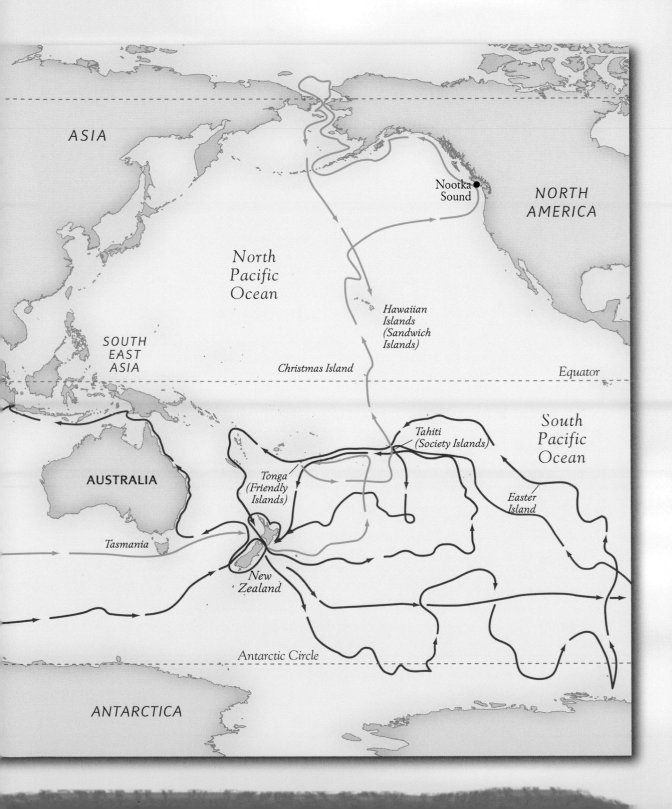

ASIA

North
Pacific
Ocean

SOUTH
EAST
ASIA

Nootka
Sound

NORTH
AMERICA

Hawaiian
Islands
(Sandwich
Islands)

Christmas Island

Equator

AUSTRALIA

Tasmania

Tonga
(Friendly
Islands)

New
Zealand

Tahiti
(Society Islands)

South
Pacific
Ocean

Easter
Island

Antarctic Circle

ANTARCTICA

Timeline

27 October 1728	James Cook is born in Yorkshire, in the north of England
1745	Cook starts work in a grocer's shop
1746	He joins the crew of a local coal-carrying ship
1755	Cook joins the Royal Navy
1762	He marries Elizabeth Batts. Later, they have six children, but only three sons grow up to be adults.
August 1768	Cook's first voyage begins as the *Endeavour* sails from Plymouth, England
September 1768	The ship anchors at Madeira
November 1768	*Endeavour* reaches Rio de Janeiro in what is now Brazil
January 1769	The ship anchors at Tierra del Fuego, at the southern tip of South America
April 1769	Tahiti (in the Society Islands) is sighted
June 1769	Cook and Green observe the Transit of Venus from Tahiti
August 1769	The search begins for the Great Southern Land
October 1769	New Zealand is sighted. Cook explores the North and South Islands.
April 1770	Australia is sighted, and the *Endeavour* anchors in Botany Bay
October 1770	The *Endeavour* arrives at Batavia, Java
July 1771	The expedition returns to Britain
July 1772	Cook's second voyage starts as the *Resolution* and *Adventure* leave Plymouth
January 1773	The first Antarctic search begins
March 1773	Arrival in New Zealand

August 1773	A stay in Tahiti
November 1773	The second Antarctic search begins
January 1774	The third Antarctic search takes place
March 1774	A visit to Easter Island
June 1774	The expedition arrives at the Tongan Islands (Friendly Islands)
July 1775	The second voyage ends with its return to Britain
July 1776	Cook's third voyage begins as the *Resolution* and *Discovery* leave Plymouth
January 1777	Arrival in New Zealand
April 1777	The ships reach the Tongan Islands
August 1777	Cook arrives at Tahiti
December 1777	A brief stop at Christmas Island
January 1778	The expedition members are the first Europeans to visit the Hawaiian Islands (Sandwich Islands)
March 1778	Exploration of the west coast of North America, with a stopover at Nootka Sound
August 1778	The ships reach the Arctic Circle, but soon have to turn back
November 1778	Arrival at Maui and Hawaii
16 January 1779	Cook decides to anchor at Kealakekua Bay, and is treated as a god
4 February 1779	The ships leaves Hawaii
8 February 1779	A storm forces a return to Hawaii
14 February 1779	Cook is attacked and killed
October 1780	The *Resolution* and *Discovery* return to Britain

Glossary

Aboriginals original people of Australia, who have lived there for thousands of years. The word "aboriginal" is also used for any people who have lived in a place for a long time.

Antarctica icy region around the South Pole

Arctic icy region around the North Pole

astronomy study of stars, planets, moons, and space

boomerang heavy curved stick used by Australian Aboriginal people for hunting animals

botany study of plants

celebrity someone who is very famous

ceremony actions, words, and often music, performed to mark a special occasion

chronometer kind of accurate clock used by sailors to help them keep time and navigate at sea

colony place that has been settled by people from another country, and which is also controlled by that country

continent one of the world's very large land masses. Europe and North America are continents.

coral tiny sea creatures whose skeletons remain after they die. Coral can be hard or soft.

dysentery very serious form of diarrhoea, when normally solid wastes become liquid and runny

Equator imaginary line around the middle of Earth, between the North and South Poles

hull main outer part or shell of a ship

inlet narrow gap or opening in a coast, which leads to a bay, river, or lake

jade hard green stone used to make ornaments and jewellery

malaria serious disease that people catch from mosquito bites. It causes great fever and sometimes death.

natural history study of plants, animals, rocks, and other things in nature

naturalist someone who studies nature

navigator someone who can steer a course across sea or land. Navigators often use maps and instruments such as compasses.

reef line of rocks or coral close to the surface of the sea

Royal Society group of scientists based in London, UK, who study topics such as astronomy and botany

scurvy disease caused by a lack of fresh fruit and vegetables in the diet

species group of animals or plants. Scientists group all living things in the natural world into species.

tornado powerful wind storm that swirls in a circle, picking up soil and other objects as it travels

zoology study of animals

Further Information

Books

Bergin, Mark and Antram, David. *You Wouldn't Want to Travel with Captain Cook!: A Voyage You'd Rather Not Make* (Franklin Watts, 2006)
A very lively description of Cook's voyages with all the gory and gruesome bits left in.

Gaines, Ann. *Captain Cook Explores the Pacific* (World History) (Enslow, 2002)
A good description of the South Pacific region, both before and after Cook's explorations.

Websites

southseas.nla.gov.au/
A large site on the South Seas, including extracts from the journals of Captain Cook, Joseph Banks, and Sydney Parkinson. The site also contains detailed clickable maps of Cook's voyages.

www.nla.gov.au/collect/treasures/mar_treasure.html
A well-illustrated website containing maps of each stage of Cook's journey and extracts from Cook's journals. There is also a section on Omai (the Tahitian) in London.

www.captcook-ne.co.uk/
A website from Captain Cook's Birthplace Museum, including a children's section with quizzes, activities, and recipes.

Places to Visit

National Maritime Museum
Park Row, Greenwich, London SE10 9NF
Tel 020 8858 4422

A museum devoted to the history of sailing, which includes navigation instruments and other objects from Cook's ships.

Pitt Rivers Museum
South Parks Road, Oxford OX1 3PP
Tel 01865 270927

The home of the Captain Cook collection of carvings, costumes, and other objects from the South Pacific.

Captain Cook's Birthplace Museum
Stewart Park, Marton, Middlesborough TS7 8AT
Tel 01642 311211

An exhibition charting the life and voyages of Captain Cook. It includes films and interactive displays.

Cambridge University Museum of Archaeology and Anthropology
Downing Street, Cambridge CB2 3DZ
Tel 01223 333516

A collection of objects collected by Cook and other explorers on their voyages to the Pacific.

Index